*craft*in*motion*

IRIS FOLDING

IRIS FOLDING

techniques for papercrafters

Eileen Goddard

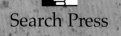

Search Press

First published in Great Britain in 2005 by
Search Press Limited
Wellwood, North Farm Road
Tunbridge Wells, Kent TN2 3DR

Reprinted 2006

Created and conceived by
Axis Publishing Ltd
8c Accommodation Road
London NW11 8ED
www.axispublishing.co.uk

Creative Director: Siân Keogh
Editorial Director: Anne Yelland
Managing Editor: Conor Kilgallon
Design: Simon de Lotz
Production: Jo Ryan, Cécile Lerbière
Photography: Mike Good

ISBN 10: 1-84448-105-0
ISBN 13: 978-1-84448-105-7

Suppliers
If you have difficulty in obtaining any of the materials and
equipment mentioned in this book, please visit the Search Press website
for details of suppliers: www.searchpress.com
Alternatively, you can write to the Publishers at the address above, for a current
list of stockists, which includes firms who operate a mail-order service.

Printed in China

Contents

An introduction to iris folding

The relatively new craft of iris folding was developed in Holland at the beginning of the millennium. It has its roots in the ecological desire to recycle, while at the same time creating something beautiful. It has many applications for hand crafters.

The first iris-folded designs were created using recycled envelopes. These tend to be discarded once the contents have been removed, but their insides are often attractive. The first folders discovered more than 300 different envelope inner designs, with more probably being added annually.

One of the first people to start iris folding must have been a patchworker, since by using paper strips – four or five different patterns to a design – a form of paper patchwork was created. These patterns had mathematical connections and are designed so that there is always a central space. The finished designs are similar to a view of the iris of a camera, hence the name, and more or less overnight a new craft was created.

Early designs were based on geometric shapes with circular, square, rectangular, triangular, and five or more sided figures all being used. Many of these shapes are still common and even more elaborate designs such as animals and birds, boats and cars, and other motifs, based on geometric combinations, have evolved.

Just as designs have developed, so too have the ranges of papers and other materials used in iris folding. Envelope strips are now used in conjunction with other papers and ribbons; binding and fabrics can also be incorporated to great effect. The earliest creations were greetings cards, and these are still probably the most common reason people choose the technique, but it can also be used in pictures and bookmarks, to embellish scrapbook pages and box lids, and in a host of other ways.

The projects in this book are intended to fire your imagination with the possibilities of the craft, as well as teaching you the basic techniques of iris folding, card making and decorating scrapbook pages. Iris folding is easy to do, requires few tools and materials to get you started, and yet the results are intricate and attractive.

As far as papers and cards go, envelope inners still provide a free source of materials while you are perfecting your technique. The number of colours and patterns is enormous. Iris folding has evolved quickly, however. You can now buy books or packs of papers specifically designed for the craft. These have the advantage that all the papers will be a similar weight and the colours and patterns will work together well. Alternatively, simply pick your own sheets of papers, and mix and match. The bigger the craft outlet, the greater your choice of styles, textures and patterns. TV and the Internet are also good sources of papers.

Holographic paper is usually used in the centre of the iris. This too is available in craft shops in individual sheets or rolls or in small packs of mixed colours. Also available from craft stores, TV,

and on the Internet are packs to make individual cards. These usually consist of a card with pre-cut aperture and backing, an envelope and enough papers to complete the iris design. If you are going to be making only the odd card for a special occasion, these can be a good idea, but if you are intending to do a lot of cards, it is more economical to buy paper in greater quantities.

You can cut your own apertures (see p. 13) in any suitable weight card. It is also possible to buy card 'blanks' with ready-cut apertures (see pp. 14–17). The drawback is that you are limited to the sizes, colours and patterns that are commercially available.

Card can be used for your iris apertures, or you can use paper and then stick this to a card for support. The variety of colours and textures is enormous, ranging from standard supplies to luxury hand-made products.

Holographic papers add impact to the centre of your iris-folded designs. These are available in a wide range of colours, patterns and textures to complement your iris papers. Start with a few standard sheets, such as silver, gold, copper, and a couple of bright colours such as red and blue.

Papers intended specifically for iris folding are available, but any good-quality papers can be mixed and matched.

You don't need a great deal of special equipment to get started in iris folding. The most important tools are a cutting mat, cutting equipment and adhesives. Avoid buying a cutting mat that is too small: if you choose an A3 size, you will be able to cut your papers and cards on it, have lengths of tape and paper strips in position as you work, and work your designs all in the same place. Many mats have grid lines printed on them, which can help you when you are ruling paper and card. A craft knife and steel rule are fine for cutting apertures and paper strips, but you will need scissors for trimming and if you intend to work with fabric. You can also buy a card trimmer with an adjustable blade to cut strips for you. Invisible tape is ideal for sticking paper strips down and low-tack tape is needed to attach templates and cards to your cutting mat, while double-sided tape is useful for sticking parts of a card together. Quick-drying PVA glue is ideal for work on narrow-bordered apertures, and for sticking other elements to your designs.

A walk around a craft store will open your eyes to the wealth of possibilities for embellishing your cards and scrapbook pages. These pages present just a small selection of the huge range of available materials.

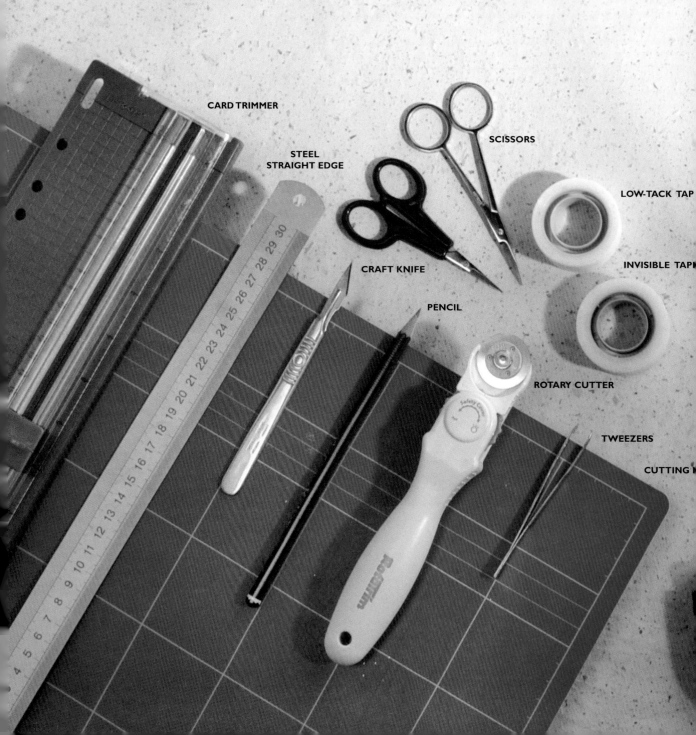

CARD TRIMMER

STEEL STRAIGHT EDGE

SCISSORS

LOW-TACK TAP

CRAFT KNIFE

INVISIBLE TAP

PENCIL

ROTARY CUTTER

TWEEZERS

CUTTING

PAPER PUNCH

PAPER PUNCH

DECORATIVE
SCISSORS

EYELETS

EYELETS

METALLIC
STICKERS

BRADS

PAPER PUNCH

PAPER PUNCH

EYELETS

EYELETS

EYELETS

GLITTER

PAPER PUNCH

PVA GLUE

CRAFT WIRE

STICKY DOT
DISPENSER

EYELET PUNCH,
HAMMER AND MAT

BEADS AND
SEQUINS

BRADS

FEATHERS

BEADS

PUNCHED
PAPER
FLOWERS

STICK-ON GEMS

BEADS

PUNCHED
PAPER SHAPES

BUGLE BEADS

BRADS

TINSEL THREAD

FABRIC BOWS

EYELETS

DECORATIVE PAPER STRIPS

SELF-ADHESIVE FLOWERS

BUTTONS

RAFFIA

GLITTER GLUE

CRAFT WIRE

SILK FLOWER

GLITTER

STICK-ON DECORATIVE FLOWERS

BRADS

METALLIC SNOWFLAKES

SILK FLOWERS

basic techniques

The basic techniques of iris folding are not difficult to learn and even a complete novice can make a successful greetings card first time.

You need to be able to cut and fold papers, to make a greetings card (or buy a card 'blank', which are widely available from craft stores) and to use a template to create your shapes. Finally you need to know how to build up an iris in a range of different shapes. Begin by making your selection of papers, choosing those of a similar weight. Follow the advice on pp. 22–23 on choosing sympathetic patterns and colourways. Set up your mat and have all your materials to hand.

preparing papers

 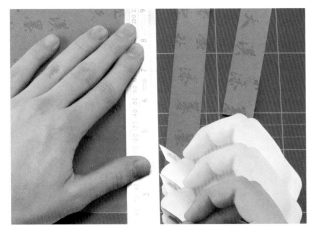

1 Place a sheet of paper on your cutting mat. Mark pencil guidelines at intervals along the paper. As a rough guide, strips for folding will be about 30–40mm (1¼–1½in) wide but this varies according to the size of card and aperture.

2 Join the pencil marks to give you a cutting line, and line up the ruler along this line. Using the craft knife, cut a paper strip. Repeat to give you enough strips of your first paper, then move to your other colours or patterns and repeat.

folding strips

 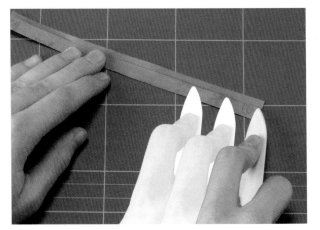

1 Take your first strip of paper and fold in one third, wrong side to wrong side. This creates a strip with half as a single layer and half as a double layer. The fold in the doubled paper will be used to create the iris.

2 Run a bone folder or your thumbnail along the fold to get a sharp crease (this is especially important with thicker papers). The sharper your creases, the better the quality of your finished irises. Repeat will all your other paper strips.

using templates – for iris shapes

1 You can buy templates to create a wealth of shapes for your cards and apertures. Hold the template in place and draw around with a pencil.

2 Use a craft knife to cut out the shape. (If you cut around the template, you risk damaging the edge with the blade.) Work smoothly, turning the paper to suit your cutting direction.

scoring and folding card

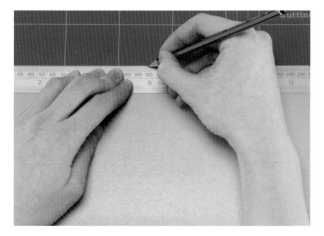

1 To make your own greetings cards, you need first to become proficient at scoring and folding. Make a light pencil mark halfway along the top of a sheet of card.

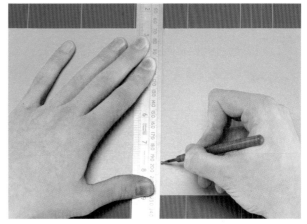

2 Make a similar mark halfway along the bottom and using a steel rule, join the two marks. Run the non-cutting edge of the craft knife blade or an embossing tool down the ruler.

3 Fold the card along the line you have scored. Use your thumbnail to get a good sharp crease. If you have a bone folder, you could use this; alternatively you could use the handle of the craft knife. The sharpness of the crease will add to the success of the card.

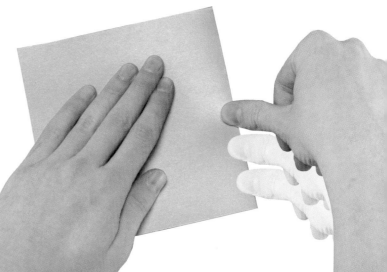

creating an iris

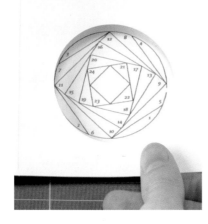

1 Choose the template you will be working and size it appropriately (see pp. 58–63). Tape it to your cutting mat and position the card aperture face down over the top. Make sure that the aperture matches the template precisely and tape it down with low-tack tape.

2 Cut and fold all your paper strips. Stick a strip of invisible tape along the length of your cutting mat and with a craft knife slice through it every 10mm (⅜in). Line up your first paper strip.

3 Lift a piece of invisible tape with the craft knife and, leaving an overlap of about 10mm (⅜in), use it to stick down the end of your strip. Line the folded edge along the guideline then, leaving a 10mm (⅜in) overlap, trim the strip.

4 Use your finger to smooth down the edge and keep it aligned, then take a strip of tape and stick the end down.

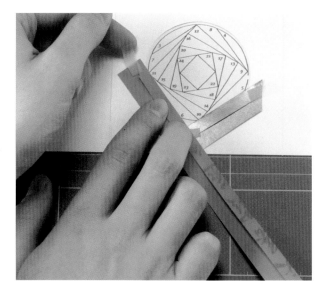

5 Take a strip of the second colour from the piles on the mat and stick the end down. Align the folded edge of this paper strip along the edge of the guideline.

6 Leaving an overlap of 10mm (⅜in), trim this strip and stick the end down. Take your third paper and leaving 10mm (⅜in) overlap stick one end down. Align and trim.

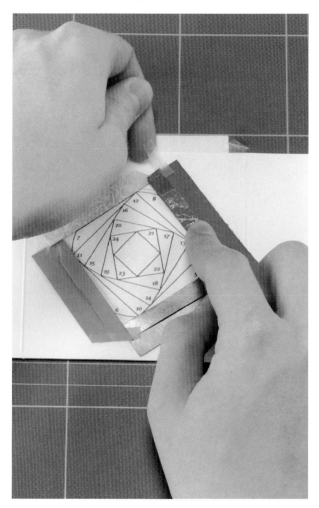

7 Take a strip of your fourth paper and stick it down using a strip of tape. Stick the tape strips well out of the way of the edge of the iris and the centre fold of the card, as shown in the photograph: this is especially important on fine designs where there is a chance of tape being visible when you reveal the finished iris. Align the folded edge of the paper strip along the guideline on the template and smooth it down.

8 Cut the strip so that there will be a 10mm (⅜in) overlap and tape it in place using a strip of invisible tape. This completes the first round of the iris.

9 Once you have worked one strip in each colour or pattern, it becomes easier to get papers in the correct order. It is still, however, worth keeping them separate on the mat.

10 Continue to add folded strips as described in steps 2 to 8, working around the template in order. Keep all strips aligned precisely on the guidelines.

TIPS

■ Take time to arrange your papers to get the best flow in terms of colour and pattern around the iris. This can be as important as the choice of papers itself.

■ When using double-sided tape on card, it is helpful to get everything positioned before you remove the backing strip. Tape your strips down, butting them at corners. Peel the backing strip from each side not more than halfway, then fold at 45° away from the centre of the card. Fold the card into position, check the alignment and press down at the corners. Then pull the remaining backing away.

11 Your final strip of paper will usually be of your fourth colour or pattern. When you have aligned papers along all edges, you will be left with a shape in the middle of the papers.

centre sparkle

1 Choose a sheet of holographic paper to complement the colours and patterns in your iris and, using scissors, cut a piece to overlap the remaining area of the template.

2 Tape this down on all four sides using strips of invisible tape. Untape the card blank and turn over to reveal the finished iris.

neatening and finishing

1 Although you were trimming the papers as you worked, when you turn over the finished iris, there are likely to be some loose ends of paper that could be trimmed further. You want as little extra bulk as possible inside the finished card, so go around with the scissors and trim off any excess.

2 Place the card with the iris face down. Like many card blanks, this one is in thirds: one third holds the actual iris, one third backs the iris, and one third forms the back of the card (where you will write your greeting). These must now be stuck together. The best material for this is double-sided tape and it needs to be applied to three edges of the card. Cut strips to fit and stick the first strip down along one edge of the card.

3 Position the second strip of tape to butt up to the end of the first. Attach the third strip, again butting up to the second. (In a square or rectangular card, the fourth side is the fold in the card, and no tape is necessary along this edge.

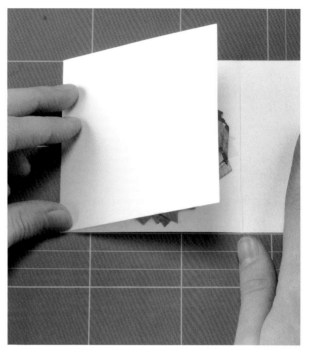

4 When you have all three strips in position, slowly remove the backing strips about halfway. as described on p. 16. This allows you to check the alignment and positioning before the tape is completely exposed.

5 Make sure that the fold line in the card is well creased, then line up the two pieces of card carefully along the back of the aperture. Card blanks are precisely cut so you should have no problems here.

6 Smooth the card down well. Run your finger along each edge in turn to ensure that the two pieces of card adhere well. This is the final part of the process.

7 Turn over your card to reveal the finished iris in position on a greetings card. Once you have mastered this basic technique, the possibilities are endless.

decorative touches

Iris-folded greetings card can be very simple, but many benefit from some form of embellishment. These are some of the more common.

Some of the finishing touches you might choose are used only in card making and in creating scrapbook pages. Others are widely used in other crafts and you may well have used some of these devices before. Peel offs and rub downs can be used in all sorts of crafts and are often an ideal finishing touch for the corners of cards decorated with fairly simple irises – an iris worked from envelope inners, for example. Peel-off strips, too, have many uses in card making.

using fine peel-off strips

1 Fine peel-off strips will fit around any shaped aperture. They are ideal if your card needs a little lift, and excellent for covering the fact that your cut aperture may not have been perfect, as they will cover the edge.

2 Stick down one end of the strip and gradually work around the aperture, sticking carefully as you go. Strips are very fine which can make them tricky to work with, but easy to lift and reposition. Cut the end using scissors and stick down.

EMBELLISHMENTS

- Do not overload a card with embellishments – they should enhance rather than detract from the iris.

- If you choose to mix and match embellishments, try to use a restricted colour palette and not too many patterns: too many colours and patterns also detract from the iris design.

- Although they look fragile, most embellishments are more robust than they appear and can be quite forgiving. They are also relatively inexpensive, so if you do make a mistake, simply take off and start again.

- Practise your technique with materials such as eyelets. Using a hammer and punch is not difficult and the more you use them, the easier it will become to strike cleanly.

using peel offs

1 Peel offs come in sheets. The back of the motif is adhesive. Lift the motif you want to use from the backing sheet using tweezers and position on the card. Rub it gently into place using your fingertips.

using eyelets

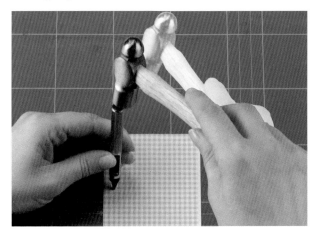

1 You cannot use the hammer and punch directly on a cutting mat as it will leave dents in it. Position the special mat under the punch (this is shown on p. 7). Position the punch and make one sharp tap with the hammer for each layer of paper or card.

2 Push the eyelet through the hole from front to back. The edges of the eyelet should sit snugly in the hole. Turn the paper over and smooth out the reverse of the eyelet using the eyelet setter.

using rub downs

1 Rub downs can be purchased in sheets. Cut off the motif you have chosen from the backing sheet, and lift into position using tweezers. Satisfy yourself that it is in the right position by eye before removing the tweezers.

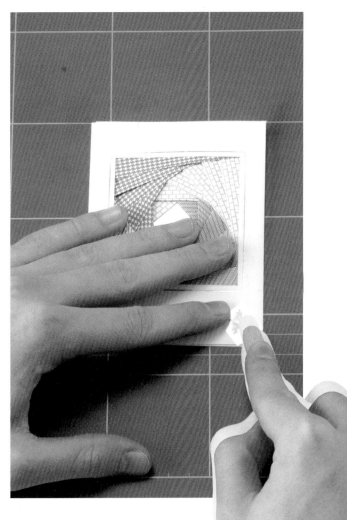

2 Place the sheet over the motif and rub down with a burnisher. This will cause the motif to adhere well to the card. Rub downs cannot be repositioned so be sure it is in the right position before burnishing. Burnish, then slowly remove the plastic backing sheet, checking that every area of the motif is well adhered.

patterns and colourways

The sheer number of patterns and colourways available in papers suitable for iris folding can be overwhelming. With so much to choose from, making a selection can be difficult.

You have two essential choices when deciding on papers – pattern and colour. You can opt to use papers with similar or related colours. Alternatively, iris papers are available in similar patterns but different colourways, such as a small floral pattern repeated in different colours. Another possibility is papers in different patterns but restricted colourways in similar tones. You also, of course, have the option of mixing plain and patterned papers in sympathetic colourways. As you make more cards and look around at those other people make, you will become more confident at choosing patterns and colours.

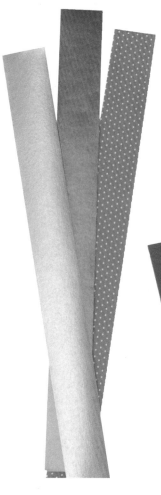

Bright oranges can be dramatic. The use of a simple striped pattern and the introduction of another colour adds impact but does not overpower. These papers would make very successful irises.

Bright and muted oranges work well together. You can apply the principle here – one dark-toned paper with two or three pale ones – to many colourways to give one side of an iris more impact.

Greens and aquas are bright and cheerful. The colours and tones are close and the patterns small and repetitive. Selections such as this do not 'fight' with each other and can make subtle cards.

Cloudy mauves such as the papers here use similar tones and patterns but a fairly restricted colour range, and with some texture. With a silver hologram, these papers would make lovely 'night sky' effect iris card.

Complementary colours such as the use of orange to complement blues and mauves, as shown here, can work well. Keep any pattern in such papers small so that the colours really make the impact.

Browns and golds in different patterns but restricted shades, are very successful. This range of colours was used for the teddy bear card shown on p. 24, but would also work on a card for a man.

Cheerful greens in similar tones with different patterns, one of which is larger than the others, are successful. Adding the yellow here spells spring, and this would be a good selection for an Easter card or spring birthday.

Subtle blues and greens in similar tones, and in small but similar repeated patterns, are often very successful. A card worked in these papers would look good with a silver centre.

Colours of autumn like the spring selection above right are effective together. A copper holographic centre would make a perfect complement to these colours and patterns.

A cute and cuddly teddy bear, a pink iris with knitted booties attached, and an off-centre sunny window with cradle offer a choice of designs for cards for babies. The templates for these cards can be found on p. 58.

cradle card

Offer these cards as congratulations on the birth of a baby or for a baby's birthday or other special occasion. In the cradle card, the iris is worked first, and then the window is stuck over it. Finally the cradle is worked and added to the card.

1 Cut an aperture in a sheet of blue card. Trace or photocopy the templates on p. 58, and cut out and use low-tack tape to fix the square template to your cutting mat. Tape the card over the template. Select, cut and fold the paper strips for the iris and lay them out in order on your mat.

2 The iris is offset in this design, so each area of the aperture is worked on separately. Start in the bottom left as you look at the aperture. This is followed by the top left. Continue to stick one end of the paper strip, trim it and stick the second end. Have strips of invisible tape ready cut and set out on your mat.

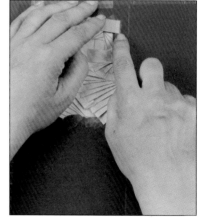

3 The bottom right of the aperture is composed of strips of yellow paper. Continue to add these to the design, remembering that you are working from the back – when you turn the design the right way up left and right will be reversed so the sun will appear top left.

4 Continue to add yellow strips, building up the design in the bottom right area. Although you do not want excessive bulk on the back of the card, it is important that there is enough overlap around the aperture to hide any ends and to hide the tape.

5 The brightest paper strips, which give an orange glow, are reserved for the top right-hand corner of the window, closest to the sun. Continue to build up the design in this area, taking care to align the edges of the paper strips along the guidelines on the template.

6 As the iris nears completion, construction reverts to a more normal pattern of working around the iris, adding one strip along each of the four edges.

7 Continue until all that remains is the centre of the iris. Cut this from a piece of gold-coloured iridescent paper. This will catch the light and shine, to represent the sun.

8 Stick the centre of the iris in place, using invisible tape. Remove the card from the cutting mat and turn over to reveal the finished iris. The iris template can also be removed from the mat.

9 Take a square of white card and using pencil and ruler mark out the window frame. Alternatively, trace or photocopy the template on p. 58.

10 Cut out the four window panes in turn and remove. Holding the craft knife at 45° to the ruler will give your panes chamfered edges.

11 Position the window frame on top of the iris and check the alignment before using a small amount of glue to stick it in place.

12 Using tracing paper and a soft pencil, trace off the cradle template from p. 58 and transfer it on to a piece of silver card. Check that all the lines are clear, and clean up any unnecessary lines. The paper strips which make up the canopy will be attached to this silver frame.

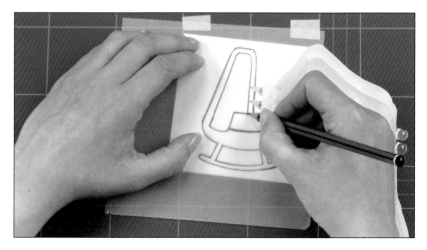

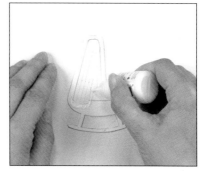

13 Carefully cut around the outline of the cradle using a craft knife, taking care to follow the lines precisely.

14 Space is limited on the canopy, which makes using tape difficult. It is easier to use glue to attach these strips. Apply a thin layer to the frame.

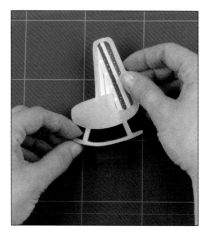

15 The paper strips for the canopy should be cut and folded as for an iris, although they will be laid into the design as overlapping strips.

16 Work from the back, as with an iris, so that the ends of all the strips will be hidden when the cradle is turned face up.

17 Check that you are happy with the striped canopy before continuing to finish off the rest of the cradle and attaching it to the card.

18 The cradle's 'blanket' is a separate piece of paper, glued in place. Use a line of glue around the edge of the paper and a dab in the centre.

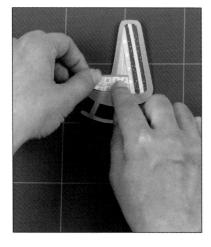

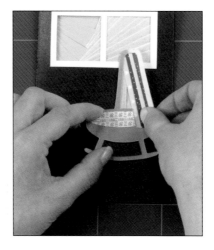

19 Check the positioning of the cradle, and when you are happy with it, use a sticky fixer to attach it to the front of the card.

A fairy princess with gauze cape and feathery wings, bright cheerful balloons and a cute tiger with iris eyes are the subjects of these cards for children. The templates for all three cards can be found on p. 59.

fairy princess card

Cards for children have to be fun. The bright balloons use an oval iris template and papers and frames in primary colours. The tiger's eyes are also ovals, with shiny offset centres. The fairy princess is every little girl's dream birthday card.

1 Cut a triangular aperture (p. 59) in the gold card. Stick the template to the cutting mat, position the triangular aperture over the template, and stick to the board using low-tack tape. Start to add paper strips in each corner.

2 The first few strips in each corner are added one after the other since the angles are too tight to start overlapping strips of papers. Once you have added these first strips, you will be able to work more conventionally.

YOU WILL NEED

cutting mat

craft knife

lightweight card: gold and purple

templates for this project, p. 59

tapes: low tack and invisible

selection of papers:
red, silver, white, pinks

PVA glue

feathers

gauze

lightweight paper: silver

2mm craft wire

sticky fixers

TIP

When folding your paper strips for the iris, you will get fairly sharp creases with your thumbnail, but for real precision, it is better to use a bone folder, or burnisher. This tool can be used for smoothing and scoring paper and card, as well as creasing.

3 You will be able to see from the template when you should start to work around the triangle, overlapping your strips of different papers. Laying your papers out on the mat in the order you will use them, and having plenty of tape strips cut as described on p. 14 will help you to work in the right order.

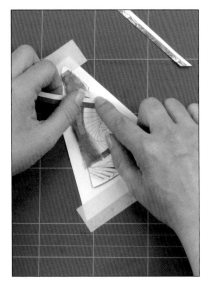

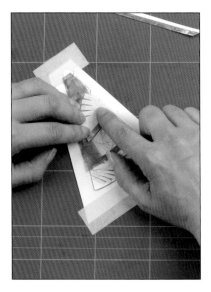

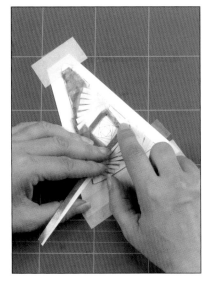

4 Work around the triangle, using a paper strip from each of your piles in turn. Work methodically, sticking one end of a strip, aligning it along the guideline on the template, leaving about 10mm overlap, trimming any excess and then sticking the second end down.

5 Smooth each strip as you work since you will not have chance to go back over it once it is partially overlapped by subsequent additions. As the design builds up, the iris will start to get bulky, so accurate trimming with minimal overlap will help to counter this.

6 'Test' each paper strip as you work to be sure you are using the correct designs. The narrower the paper strips and more complex the design, the easier it is to make mistakes. It is frustrating to get to the end of a fiddly design to find that it has not worked as planned.

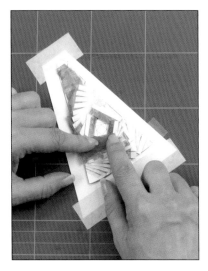

7 Continue to build up the design. As you get closer to the centre, the strips get shorter, and even greater precision is necessary when placing them along the lines on the template.

8 When you have covered every area of the template, cut a shiny piece of red paper for the centre of the iris and stick it in place using invisible tape. Clear the mat of any papers you have left.

9 Carefully detach the iris from the cutting mat and turn over to reveal the finished design.

10 Trace the template for the wings on p. 59, transfer it to white paper, and cut out.

11 Score the folds with the blunt edge of the knife. Starting in the centre and working outwards in both directions, fold the paper back and forwards along the pencil lines so that the wings are creased along their length.

12 The central area of the wings will be covered by the princess iris, but the wings fan out to give the illusion that the princess is flying through the air.

13 Using a small amount of glue, attach feathers to the front of the wings. Position the 'ribs' of the feathers in the centre so that they will be hidden.

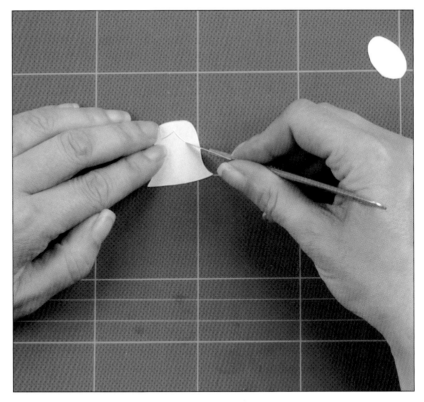

14 Use the bell-shaped template (p. 59) as your pattern for the princess's hair, and cut this out of gold card, using the craft knife. Glue the hair behind the top of the triangle.

15 Cut an oval face for the princess and glue this on top of the hair and to cover the point of the triangular body. The face will look as if it is sitting on top of the shoulders.

16 Place the wings right side up on the cutting mat and apply a small amount of glue to the back of the iris, at around shoulder level. Then stick the iris body to the wings.

17 Using the template on p. 59, cut two feet and two hands from gold card. Attach the feet from the back so that they protrude from the gown's hem.

18 Glue the princess's left hand in place: the right one must be attached once the wand is in place. Then cut a silver crown and glue that to the top of her head to sit in her hair.

19 Use glue to attach a gauze cape to the back of the wings. Stick a silver star to the end of the 2mm craft wire wand, then apply a spot of glue to the right hand of the wire and stick the wand in place. Glue the princess's right hand on to the wire, to cover its end.

20 Glue the glittery silver inset on to the card, then use sticky fixers to attach the princess to the card.

An iridescent butterfly, bright sunflowers and trendy shopping bags are the subjects for cards for female friends and relatives, for birthdays and other special occasions. The templates for these three cards can be found on p. 60.

sunflowers card

These cards are suitable for birthdays and other special occasions for women. The shopping bag uses a square design, and the lower wings of the butterfly are based on triangular irises. The sunflowers use a circular template, with the iris in the centre.

1 Cut four sunflower heads from yellow card, using the template on p. 60. Since each flowerhead is going to be composed of two rounds of yellow petals offset, the design is not too complicated – no more than ten petals. Cut out the centre, then cut around the petals carefully with a craft knife.

2 Using low-tack tape, attach the template for the iris (p. 60) to your cutting mat, then tape your first flowerhead on top with the centre of the flowerhead positioned so that the iris is in its centre. Cut and fold your strips for the iris and arrange them on your cutting mat. Start to stick down your iris strips.

YOU WILL NEED

craft knife
■
cutting mat
■
lightweight card:
yellow, green and cream
■
templates for this project, p. 60
■
tapes: low tack and invisible
■
selection of papers:
creams, browns and golds
■
scissors
■
PVA glue
■
lightweight paper:
beige
■
sticky fixers

3 Work around the template, sticking your strips down in order. Use small strips of invisible tape – glue does not dry quickly enough and can 'seep' through fine papers and stain. Allow approximately 10mm overlap at the end of each strip.

4 Trim each strip using scissors. Trimming as you go prevents the iris from getting too bulky, and gives you a clearer view of the template and of how the design is working. Take care to align the edge of each strip with the guideline on the template.

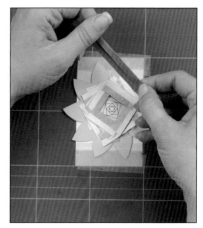

5 The papers used for the outermost parts of the iris are paler in colour than those used towards the iris itself to mimic sunflowers in nature, where the very centre of the flower is the darkest part. Check a paper is in the correct order before sticking it down.

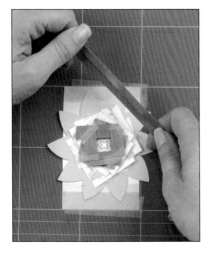

6 As you get closer to the centre of the iris, the strips get shorter. It is important to be sure that you follow the guidelines closely at this stage.

7 When you have added all the strips, and the central motif, detach the flowerhead from the template, and start on the second flower.

8 Follow the same order of working as for the first flower, using the paper strips in the same colour order. Work logically around, sticking one end, trimming off the excess, then sticking down the second end.

9 Detach the second flowerhead from the template and turn over to reveal the finished iris. Check that everything is in the correct place. At this stage, you can detach the template from your mat, as you will not need it again for this card.

10 Using the non-cutting edge of the craft knife blade, carefully score a centre line down each petal of the second set of petals for both flowers.

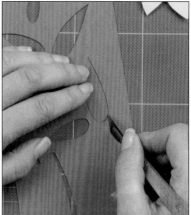

11 Cut a series of leaf shapes from the green card, using the craft knife. Use the template on p. 60 as a guide for these. The leaves have one pointed end and one flat one.

12 Fold each petal in turn along the line you have scored. This will give this second round of petals a more three-dimensional quality than the first and add depth to the finished flowers. Work around each flowerhead in turn.

13 Run a thin line of glue around the centre of the petals. Avoid the very edge so that glue does not seep out on to the irises, and don't stray into the areas you have folded. Glue with a fine nozzle will help with this.

14 Stick the second round of petals over the first, taking care to match the centres exactly. If they don't line.up you will obscure part of the iris.

15 Cut stalks from the green card using the template on p. 60. Stick to the back of the flowerheads using invisible tape. Don't worry about length at this point: you can trim them later.

16 Using the non-cutting edge of the craft knife blade, carefully score a centre line on each leaf. With your thumbnail, crease each leaf in turn along the scored line and allow to open again.

17 Start placing the leaves along the stalks. It helps to place them all by eye first, before you start gluing. Once you are happy with the visual arrangement, use a small dab of glue on the 'flat' end of each leaf to stick it to the back of the stalk. Glue the leaves at about 45° to the stalk.

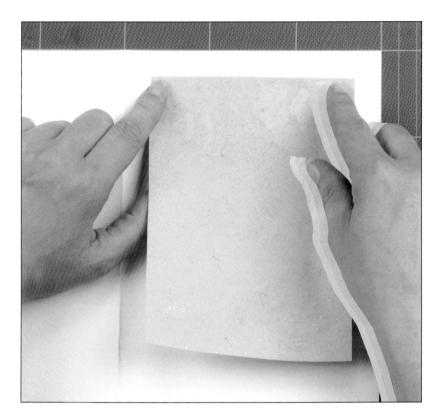

18 Select papers for the card and for the inset. Centre the inset over the front of the card, leaving a more generous margin at the bottom than at the top and sides and glue in place.

19 Position the first flower and stalk on the front of the card. For balance and to add visual interest, allow the petals to 'break out' of the inset paper. It is easier to finalize the position of all the finished elements before you start to stick them in place.

20 Place the second flowerhead slightly below and to the left of the first, as you are looking at the card. Use a thin coating of glue to attach the stalks of both flowers, but the leaves should not be stuck down: leave them to stand out from the card to balance the texture in the flowerheads and add to the three-dimensional quality of the finished card. Try to avoid overlapping the petals so that each flowerhead is clearly visible; the leaves can overlap.

21 Attach the flowerheads to the card using sticky fixers which will support the weight of the flowers. Use two or three on top of one another for added height. Trim off any overhanging stalk, using the craft knife.

A seafaring theme featuring an iris porthole, a car coming down the road from the centre of the scenic square iris and a three-dimensional golfing scene are the subjects of cards for men. The templates for these three cards can be found on p. 61.

golf card

These three cards demonstrate that cards for male friends and relatives do not have to be in the least boring. All are based on simple iris shapes, but enhanced with additional details for heightened impact.

YOU WILL NEED

cutting mat

■

lightweight card: cream

■

selection of papers: blue, pale green, grass green, whites and creams for the iris, silver holographic, pearlescent light and dark green, yellow

■

PVA glue

■

scissors

■

craft knife

■

templates for this project, p. 61

■

tapes: low tack, invisible, double-sided

■

cocktail stick

1 This card is made in several layers to give it depth and to differentiate sky, rough, green and fairway. Cut a piece of card the size of your finished card. This gives you something to glue subsequent layers of paper to – the papers themselves do not have enough stability. Tear a piece of paper for the sky.

2 For a more outdoor feel, the papers for the rough and fairway, in addition to the sky, are torn rather than cut. This also gives a good texture to the card. The papers you use for these areas need to be fairly light so that you do get a good torn edge: thicker papers work less successfully.

3 Glue the torn pale green fairway strip on top of the sky. Smooth it down with your fingers to get rid of any air bubbles and ensure good adhesion. Then trim the overlap with the craft knife or scissors so that it is flush with the edges of your backing card.

4 Tear off a larger piece of green paper for the rough in which the golf ball iris will lie. Again tearing rather than cutting gives texture to the paper, adds to the illusion of depth and will enhance the three-dimensional quality of the finished card.

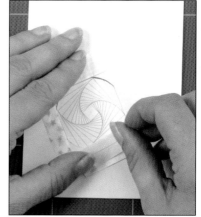

5 Tape the circular iris template (p. 61) to your cutting mat. Cut an aperture the same size as the iris template in the bottom right of your card. Stick this over the iris template, matching the edges precisely. Prepare your iris strips and place them on the cutting mat.

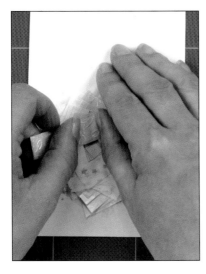

6 Start making the iris. In this design there are four different papers in varying shades, patterns and textures of white and cream.

7 Work around the design, aligning the edges of the paper strips along the guidelines on the template.

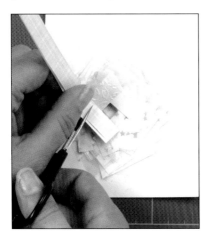

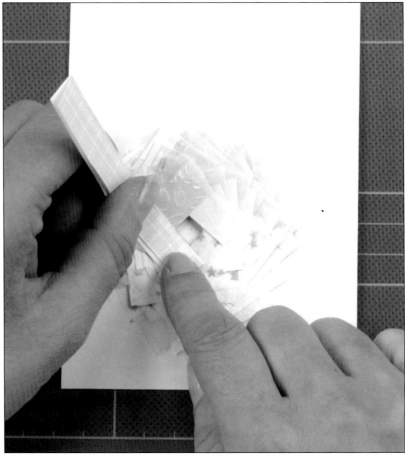

8 Stick one end of each strip down, and align it along the guideline. Leave about 10mm overlap, then trim the strip using scissors. Stick the second end down, then move on to the next strip, following the template.

9 Work around your iris, adding one strip at a time from each of your piles of paper strips. Smooth them down as you work as once the next strip is in place, it is difficult to do this successfully, The fold lines should look crisp.

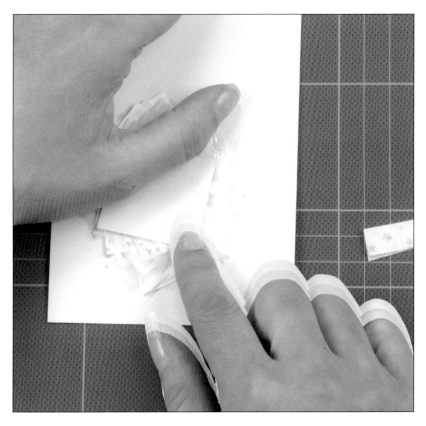

10 Choose a silver holographic paper for the centre of the iris and cut this using scissors.

11 Continue adding your iris strips until there is only the central square left to fill. Stick your holographic paper into place using invisible tape. This will draw the eye into the centre of the golf ball.

12 Cut an oval into the light green area of the design for the green. This is too narrow for an iris but can still be made to resemble the green by using alternate light and dark green strips.

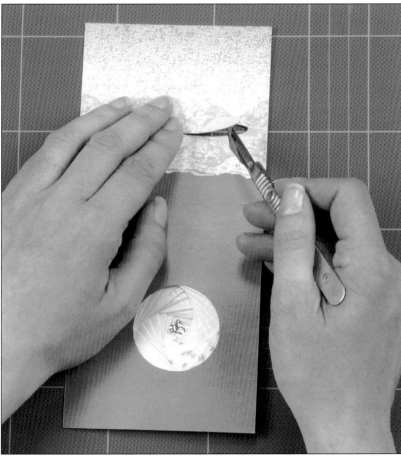

13 Cut and fold strips for the green exactly as you do for iris strips, although these will be added to the card in stripes, rather than as you would work around an iris.

14 Work from the back of the card and position the strips of paper for the green.

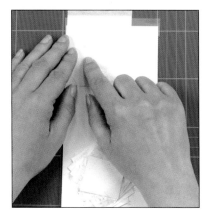

15 Tape these strips in place at each end, exactly as you would do for iris strips. Overlap the strips slightly, keeping everything evenly spaced.

16 The finished iris golf ball sits in a circular hole cut into the green grass near the bottom of the card.

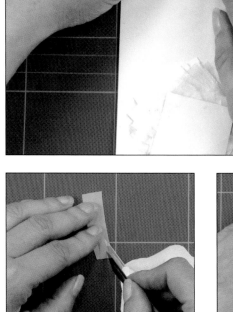

17 Cut blades of grass from the green paper. These have pointed tips and flat bases.

18 Carefully, using the non-cutting edge of the craft knife, score a centre line down each blade of grass.

19 Fold the long blades of grass along the scored lines to crease them. This will add depth to the card.

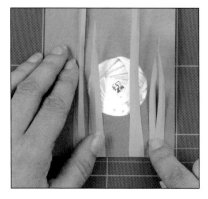

20 Position the blades of grass by eye, until you get a pleasing arrangement, partially obscuring the iris.

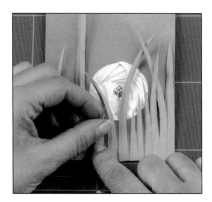

21 Glue the base of each blade of grass to the card, leaving the top of the blades unattached, to add texture.

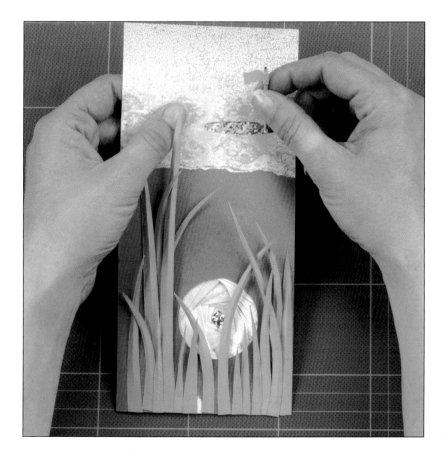

22 Glue bright yellow paper around half a cocktail stick and position on the green. Apply glue to the back of the flag and stick to the card.

23 Fold the card you have selected for your mount into three and cut an aperture to hold the scene into the central third.

24 Attach a strip of double-sided tape along all four edges of the aperture, then attach the golfing scene. Press down with your fingertips.

25 Add double-sided tape to all four edges of the aperture, which now includes the scene, and fold the backing over. Peel the backing from the tape and secure the inside of the card.

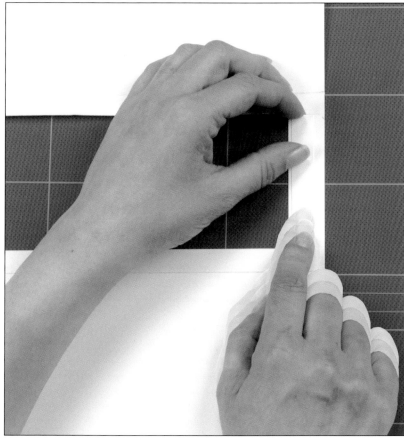

A colourful cocktail glass can be offered for any birthday or anniversary celebration, while red hearts are clearly for Valentine's day. Dark bats and pumpkins spell Halloween, while a tree is indicative of Christmas. The templates for these cards can be found on p. 62.

halloween card

The Christmas tree and the cocktail glass here are based on triangular irises, and the Valentine's day card uses a heart-shaped iris. The Halloween card is a simple square iris, with drama created through the use of colour, texture and the offset iris.

1 Cut a square aperture in a sheet of dark blue card. Tape the square iris template (p. 62) to your cutting mat using low-tack tape and position the card so that the centre of the iris is offset to the left as you look at it. Tape the card to your mat and start to fill in the bottom.

2 Because the iris is offset, you will have to fill in the bottom of the card first, before you can start to move around the aperture overlapping the strips. Tape one end down, align the strip along the guideline on the template, cut off excess paper, and tape down.

YOU WILL NEED

cutting mat
■
craft knife
■
card: dark blue, orange, green
■
templates for this project, p. 62
■
tapes: low tack, invisible, double-sided
■
papers: blue and purple iris papers, pearlescent white, pearlescent black, matt black
■
glue
■
sticky fixers

3 Start to add strips to the left as you look at the card. Like the first strips, these are fairly broad. Follow the guidelines on the template for order of working. Since the papers here are similar in tone, keeping them on different areas of the mat is a good idea.

TIP

Have plenty of tape strips cut and ready for use on your cutting mat. The easiest way to do this is to tape a strip about 150mm long to your mat and slice through it at approximately 5mm intervals with your craft knife. Lift the strips one by one as you need them using the craft knife blade.

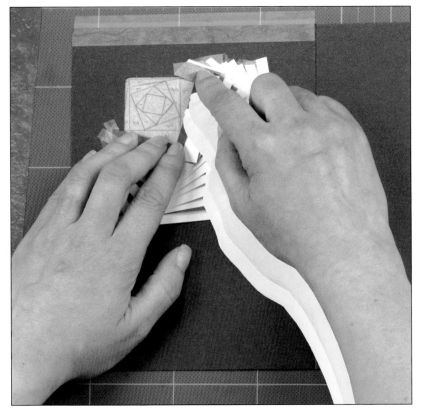

4 When you get to the appropriate point on the template, start to add strips of your third paper, overlapping the three papers as you work.

5 The three papers are used in most of the iris: it is only when you are nearly finished that the fourth is added.

6 Once you have started to use all four papers, you can work the iris conventionally, one strip of each type in order around the template. Continue to follow the guidelines, aligning the edge of each strip with the lines on the template, and sticking and trimming as you work.

7 Work around the iris, gradually filling it in. As you add each strip, smooth it down with your thumbnail to make sure that it is crisply folded. This will result in a better crafted finished card.

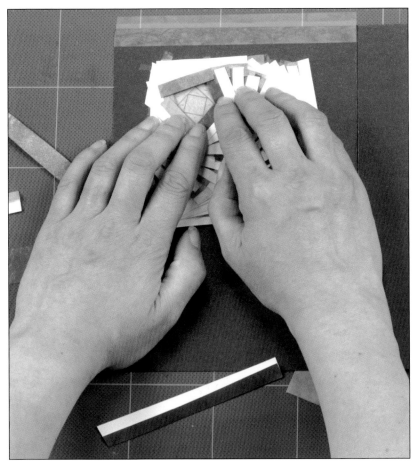

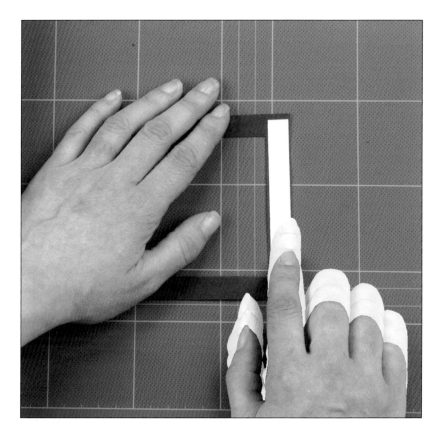

8 The centre of the iris is cut from a piece of glittery silvery-white paper, to look like the moon. Stick in place using invisible tape.

9 Frame the iris window using sparkly black paper. Using the template on p. 00, cut a square frame to match the dimensions of the aperture and approximately 15mm deep on all sides.

10 Check the frame against the aperture, then use double-sided tape to attach it. To position the frame and adjust if necessary, peel back 6cm from the top strip. On each side, fold at right angles to the main strip. Turn the frame over and place in position. Peel off the tape carefully and smooth down.

11 Use black paper for the bats. Cut these out using a craft knife, following the templates on p. 62. These will add drama to the card.

12 Use a dab of glue to stick the bats in place. Position the smallest ones at the top of the iris window to suggest the illusion of distance.

13 Allow the largest bat to break out of the window and glue it on the card itself. This gives the impression that the bats are flying out of the window to spook the viewer.

14 As you glue each bat in place, smooth it down with your fingers so that there are no creases in the paper. As long as you have used the minimum amount of glue necessary, there will not be any seepage.

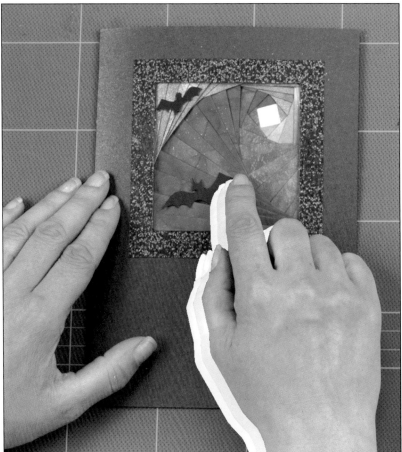

15 Using the templates on p. 62, cut an oval from a piece of orange card, then cut three banana-shaped pieces and glue on to the pumpkin to look like segments. Cut out triangular eyes and nose, and a zigzag mouth.

16 Using the craft knife, cut the stalk for the pumpkin from a piece of card, then glue it to the top of the pumpkin from the back.

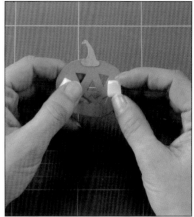

17 Attach two sticky fixers one on top of the other to each side of the back of the pumpkin. Doubling up on sticky fixers in this way adds greater depth to the overall design.

18 Check the positioning of the pumpkin by eye before you peel the backing off the sticky fixers. It sits across the border of the iris, but does not obscure any part of the iris itself.

19 Peel the backing from the sticky fixers and attach the pumpkin to the card. The card is now complete. This would make an ideal invitation to a Halloween trick or treat party, and is suitable for adults and children alike.

Scrapbook pages lend themselves to many decorative elements, including iris folding, brads, eyelets and other motifs. Choose an appropriate iris for the theme. The templates for these irises can be found on p. 63.

baby scrapbook page

Scrapbooks are places for treasured possessions and memories. An iris-folded shell design adorns the holiday-themed page, while an iris butterfly enhances the garden page. A circular iris rattle is included on the baby page.

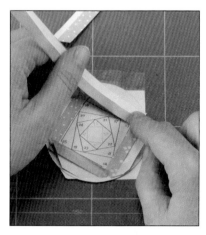

YOU WILL NEED

craft knife

■

cutting mat

■

templates for this project, p. 63

lightweight card: pink, gold

■

tapes: low-tack, invisible, double-sided

selection of papers: pink for iris, holographic for iris centre, decorative papers for frames and borders

■

scissors

■

PVA glue

■

spray adhesive

■

scrapbook page, 30 x 30cm (12 x 12in)

■

baby photograph

sticky fixers

sticky dots

acetate

■

double-sided foam fixer strip

■

eyelet punch, hammer and eyelets

■

decorative flowers and feet brads

■

decorative tinsel thread

■

border punch

■

feather

1 The 'head' of the rattle is framed with pink card. Using the craft knife, cut a frame from a sheet of card using the template on p. 63. Tape the circular iris template to your cutting mat, align the card along the edges of the template and using low-tack tape, tape the pink frame face down over the iris template.

2 Cut and fold your iris papers as described on p. 12. These are in four shades and patterns of pinks. Place the strips in the order you will use them on the cutting mat, so that once you get started on the design everything is to hand and logically arranged. Work the first strip in each paper.

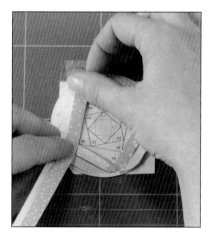

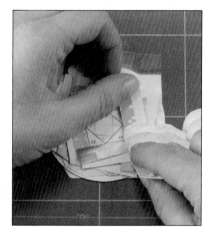

3 Leaving approximately 10mm overlap, stick one end of a strip down with invisible tape. Align the strip along the guideline on the template, leave 10mm overlap at the other end, and trim off using scissors. Stick this end down with invisible tape.

4 Continue around the iris, using your strips in turn, according to the guidelines on the template. Smooth each strip down as you attach it so that all the folded edges on the finished iris will look sharp. This design is fairly small, so should not take long to complete.

TIP

When sticking large areas of paper to pages, use spray adhesive or sticky dots rather than glue as glues can cause air bubbles which can be difficult to remove.

5 Work around the iris in order until you have reached the centre. For this design, a shiny pink holographic paper is used as the central motif. Cut a piece of this to size using scissors and stick it face down in the central area using strips of invisible tape.

6 Untape the rattle head and turn over to reveal the finished iris design. You can also remove the iris template from your mat at this stage.

7 Using the template on p. 63, trace the handle of the rattle on to gold card and, following the guidelines, cut out using the craft knife.

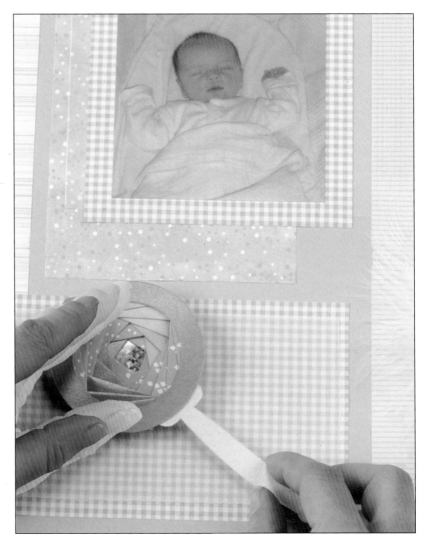

8 Attach the handle to the rattle using a small amount of glue. Add two vertical strips of paper to frame the page, and stick down backing frames for the photograph and rattle. Add the baby's photograph.

9 Stack three sticky fixers to the handle of the rattle, and three more to its head, peel off the backing and stick the rattle on to the scrapbook page. Stacking sticky fixers in this way means that the rattle sits proud of the page.

10 Cut four heart shapes from the pink card you used for the rattle head, one for each corner of the frame for the 'shaker' picture.

11 Use sticky dots to attach these to the corners of the frame, leaving a tiny margin between the heart and the aperture in the frame. Press down with your fingers.

12 Punch out teardrop shapes of pink papers. Cut two pieces of acetate slightly smaller than the frame.

13 Stick one piece of acetate to the back of the frame using double-sided tape. Check you have enough teardrops, then attach a strip of double-sided sticky foam fixer to the acetate on all four sides. Unpeel three sides and stick on the second piece of acetate. Insert the teardrops through the fourth side, unpeel the backing and stick.

14 Run your fingertip along the sides of the frame to be sure the frame and shaker picture are stuck together, otherwise your teardrops may fall out.

15 Check the position of the framed image on the page by eye. If you are satisfied apply two sticky fixers to each corner of the frame and stick it in place on the page.

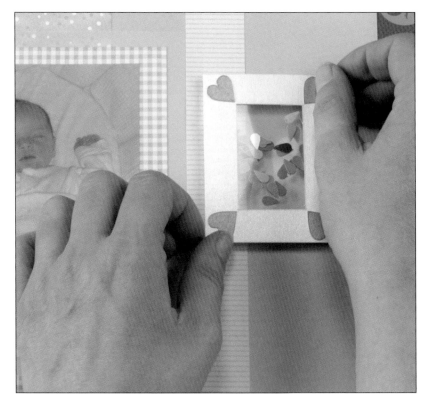

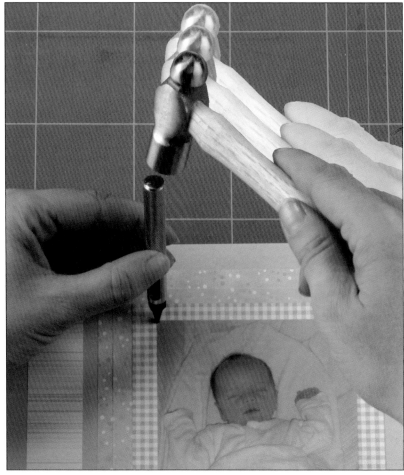

16 Using the hammer and punch create a hole in each corner of the frame of the baby's photograph. Position them so that each flower brad overlaps the corner of the baby's photograph slightly to add visual interest.

17 Push the flowers through the holes you have created. Punch similar holes for the foot brads along the left-hand side of the page, and push three pairs of feet through these holes, as if the baby is walking up the page.

18 Get the wings of the brads as flat as possible and stick a piece of invisible tape over them to prevent damage to any other scrapbook page. Pages usually back on to one another.

TIP

Avoid the temptation to overload scrapbook pages with additional decorative elements: in general, the more you add the greater the chance that you will start to detract from the main aim, which is usually to showcase family celebrations and achievements. The photographs of family members, holiday locations or other significant places, should always dominate, with other elements enhancing rather than detracting from them.

19 Use an eyelet punch and hammer to attach three eyelets on the backing paper of the rattle, and four to the vertical strip on the right of the page. Glue a decorative rope of pink and silver 'tinsel' across the top of the page.

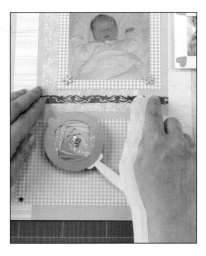

20 Cut a strip of paper, then use a border punch to get a decorative pattern. Attach to the page with sticky dots. To finish, punch two holes and, using a strip of tinsel thread, tie a feather to the page.

You can trace the templates on these pages for use in making your own cards and scrapbook pages. Alternatively you can photocopy them, or enlarge or reduce them on a photocopier. If you do change the size, remember to enlarge or reduce every relevant template.

babies' cards

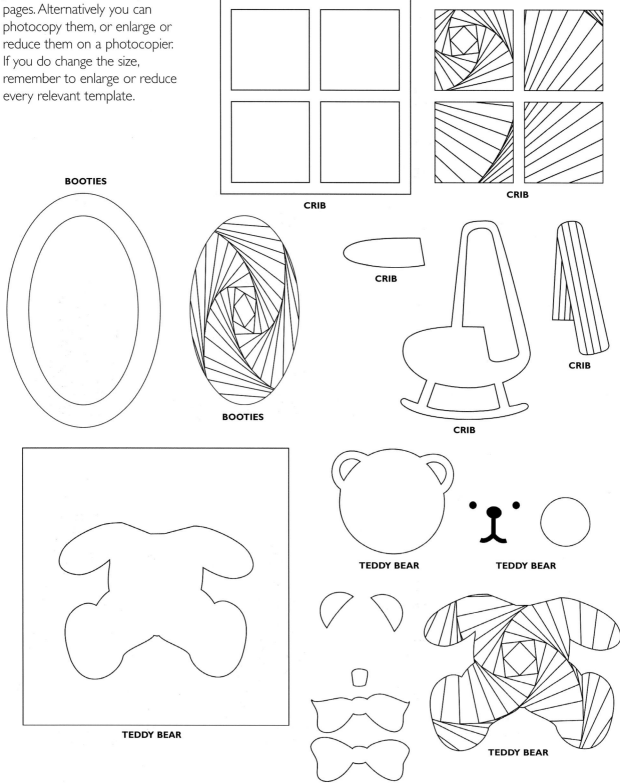

BOOTIES

CRIB

CRIB

CRIB

BOOTIES

CRIB

CRIB

TEDDY BEAR

TEDDY BEAR

TEDDY BEAR

TEDDY BEAR

TEDDY BEAR

children's cards

TIGER

BALLOON

TIGER

BALLOON

TIGER

FAIRY PRINCESS

FAIRY PRINCESS

FAIRY PRINCESS

FAIRY PRINCESS

FAIRY PRINCESS

women's cards

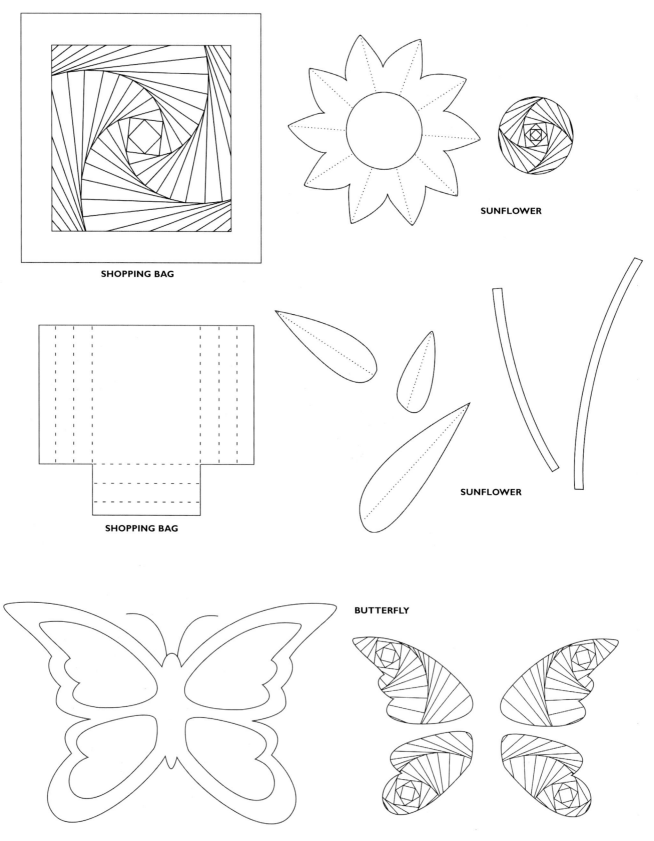

SHOPPING BAG

SUNFLOWER

SHOPPING BAG

SUNFLOWER

BUTTERFLY

men's cards

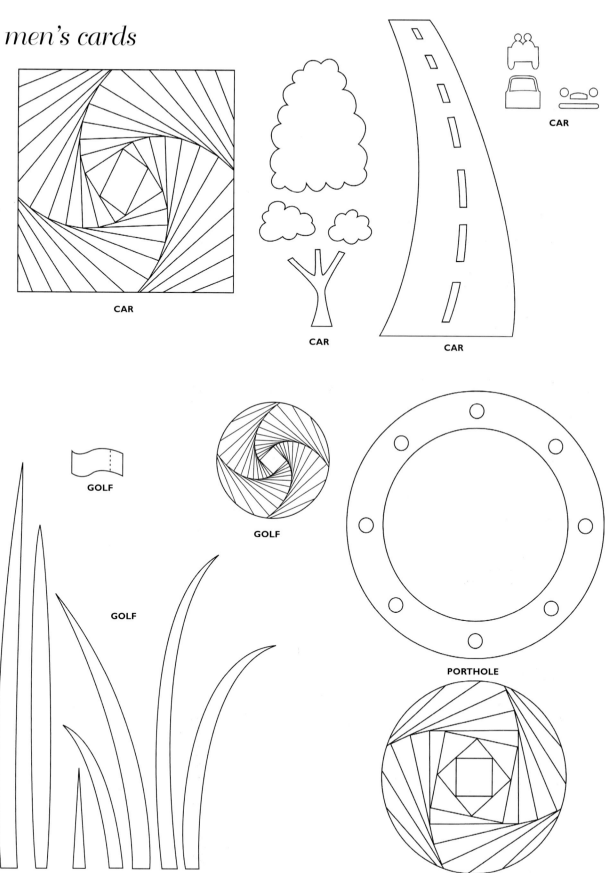

CAR

CAR

CAR

CAR

GOLF

GOLF

GOLF

PORTHOLE

special occasions

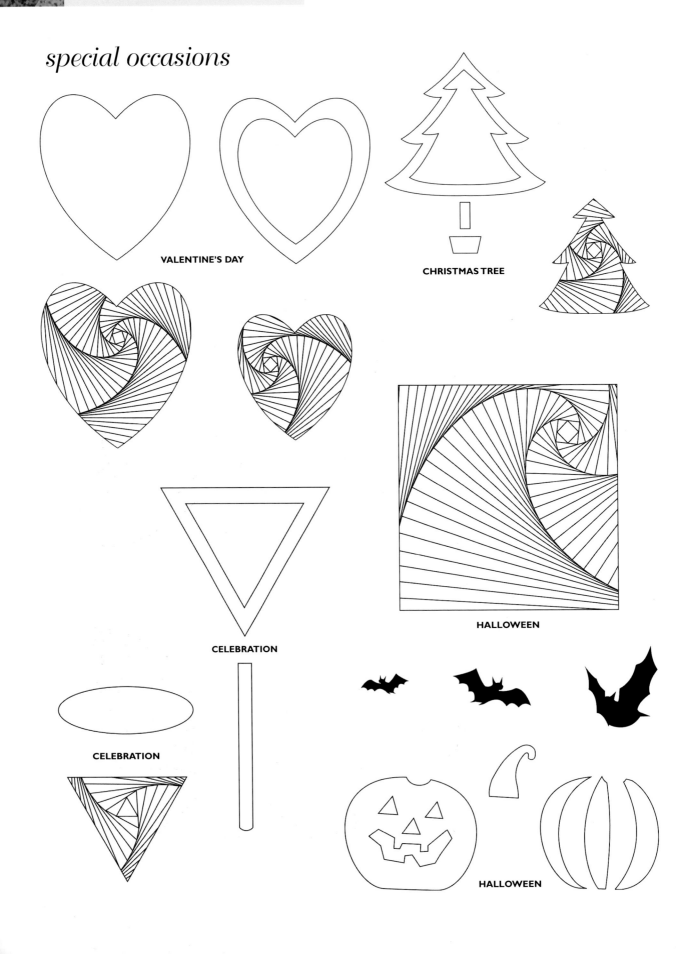

VALENTINE'S DAY

CHRISTMAS TREE

CELEBRATION

HALLOWEEN

CELEBRATION

HALLOWEEN

scrapbook pages

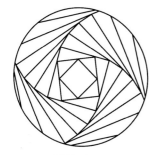

NEW BABY

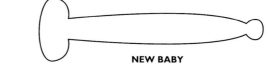

NEW BABY

NEW BABY

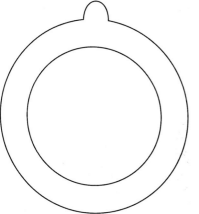

GARDEN

HOLIDAY

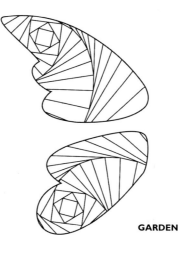

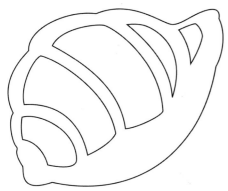

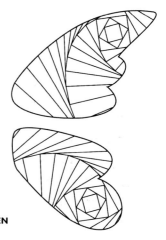

GARDEN

index

acknowledgement

The author would like to thank Priory Methodist Craft Club, Bedford.